Hi, kids! It's your pal, Eleanor. My friends and I are going to take a trip to the carnival. Come join us.

Look at these stickers! Every time you learn something new, you get a star sticker. When you finish each section, you'll get a special train sticker to put on your Certificate of Completion at the end of the book.

One more thing! When you see this picture, it means I am there to give you a little help! Just look for **Eleanor's Tips**.

Are you ready? Let's go!

Eleanor's Tips

You have **five** fingers on each hand. Count them— 1, 2, 3, 4, 5!

We're off to the Number Carousel. Help us find our way!

Start at our train. Draw a line along the tracks, following the numbers in order from one to five. Then color in those numbers.

| 1 | 2 | 3 | 4 | 5 |

All of these carousels are so much fun!

Connect the dots on my ticket to find out which carousel we'll ride! Circle that carousel.

1　　　　**2**　　　　**3**

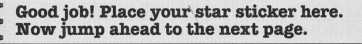

Eleanor's Tips

To make the number **4**, you have to lift your pencil off the paper once. Trace the arrows with your finger to make the number 4.

I read about this  in my 📖. Which path should we take to get there?

Color in the path that shows the numbers in order from 1 to 10.

1 2 3 4 5 6 7 8 9 10

8   3
9   5   1
10
2
4
6
7
10

1
2
3
4
5
6   7   8   9
1   6   4   3   5

2
7
10
9
8

I know what I want to ride on.

Connect the dots from 1 to 10 to see what it is. Then color it in.

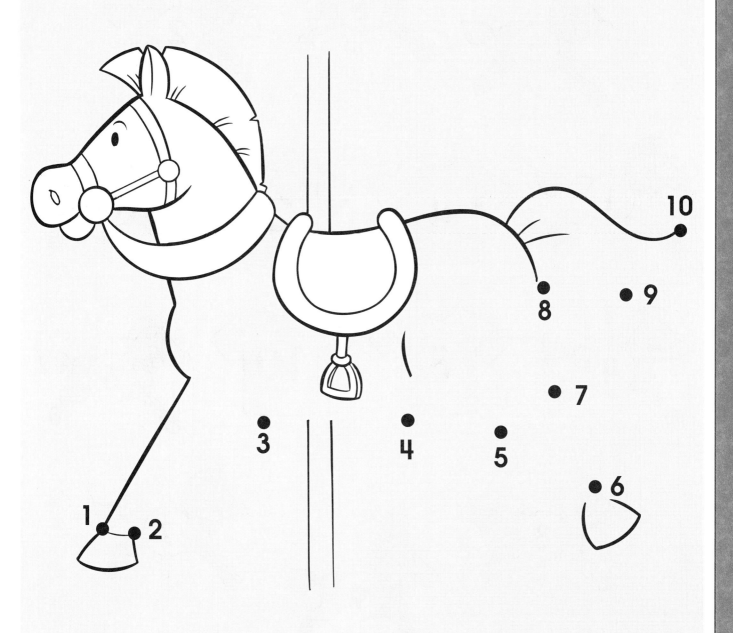

Do you like our number shirts?

Draw lines to connect the numbers on our shirts to the matching 🐎's.

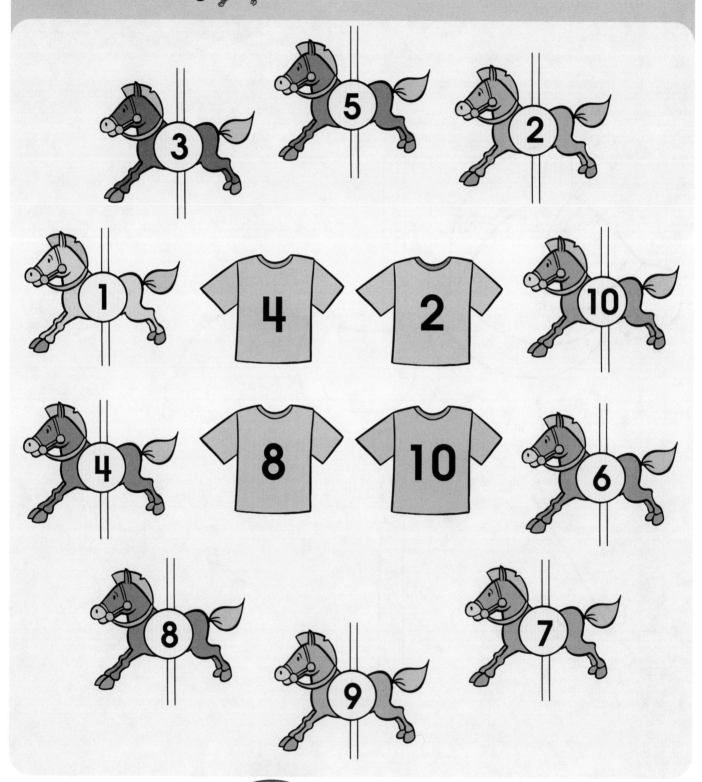

When I close my eyes I pretend I'm riding on a real 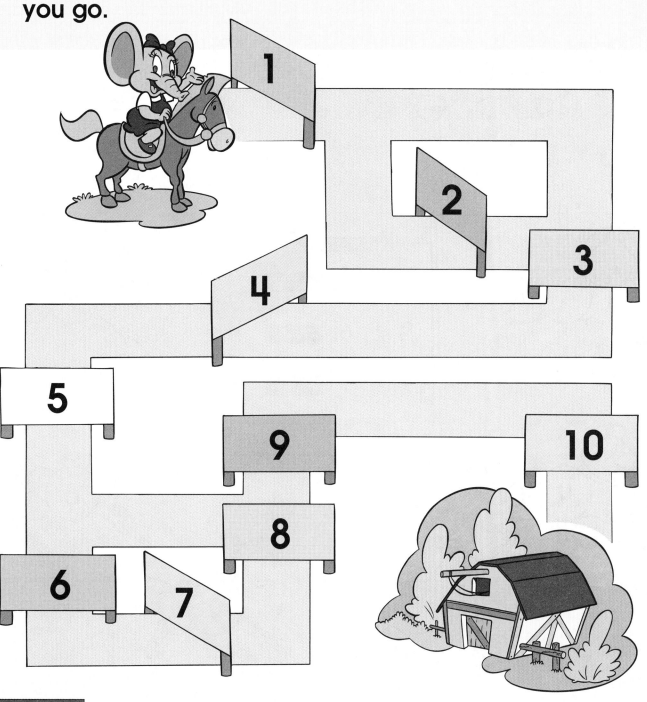 and jumping fences! Help my horse find her way back to the barn.

Draw a line along the path that shows the numbers in order from 1 to 10. Say the numbers out loud as you go.

Nice work! Place your star sticker here. Now jump ahead to the next page.

Follow the Numbers 7

Kisha wants to paint a picture.

Help her color the 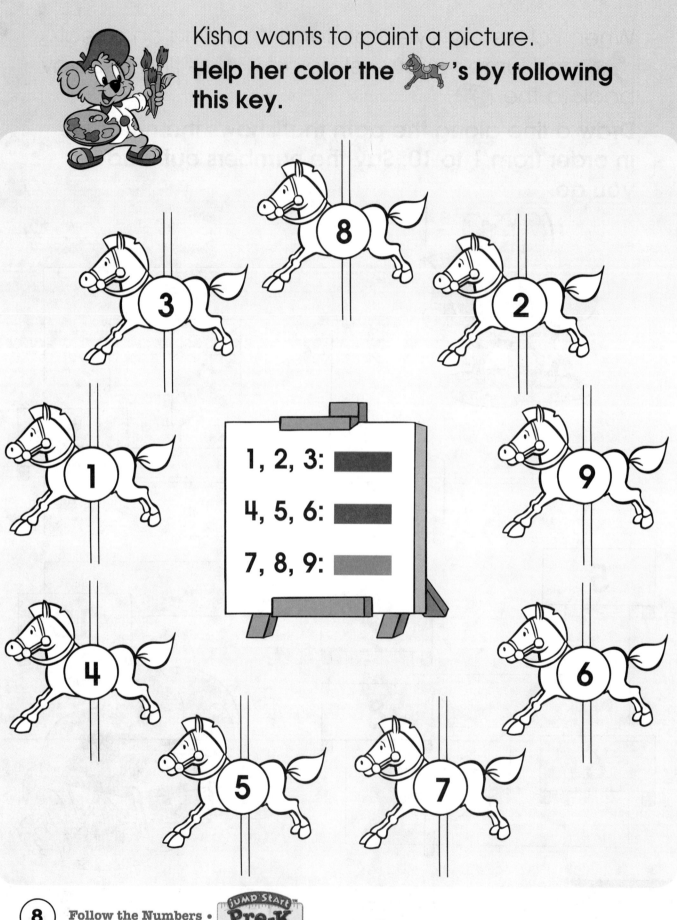's by following this key.

1, 2, 3: ▬

4, 5, 6: ▬

7, 8, 9: ▬

There's someone silly near the .

Connect the dots from 1 to 20 to find out who it is! Then color him in.

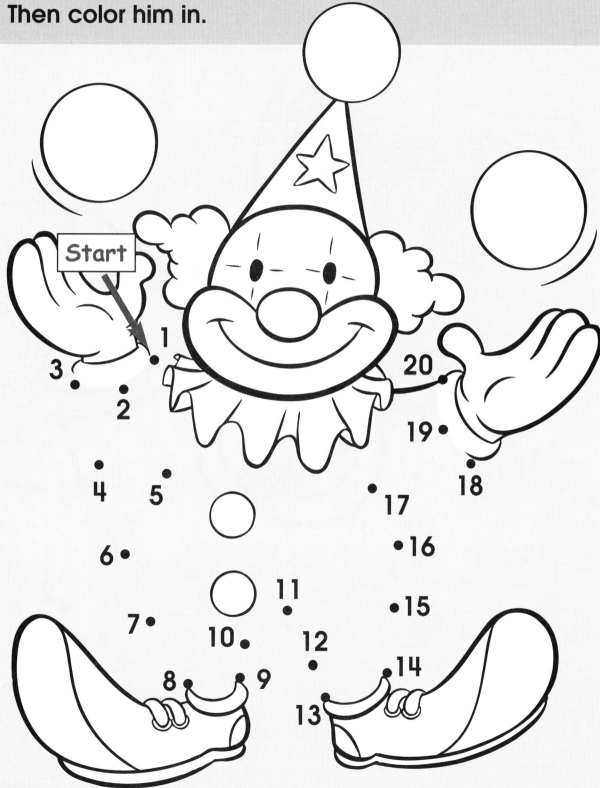

Great job! Place your star sticker here. Jump ahead to see what you've learned.

Follow the Numbers **9**

Let's pretend we're flying on our carousel 's!

Put your pencil on the number 1 on my horse and connect the dots from 1 to 20.

Then put your pencil on the number 1 below and connect the dots from 1 to 10. Now I can ride on my horse and you can color in the pictures!

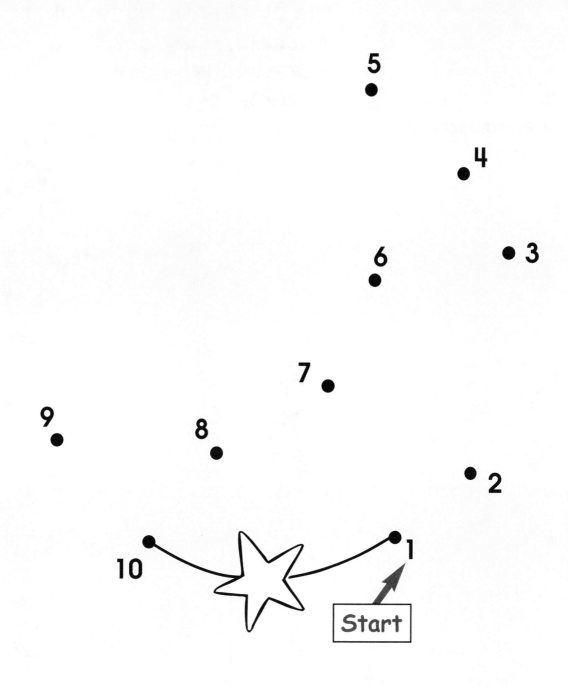

Excellent! Place a train sticker on your Certificate of Completion. Now jump ahead for more fun.

Review 11

Eleanor's Tips

Just like letters, numbers go in a certain order, or **sequence**.

We're off to play with the , but Kisha needs a ticket first.

Help her by tracing the number on her ticket. Say the number on each ticket out loud, starting with Eleanor. Then color in each ticket.

1   2   **3**   **4**   **5**

The 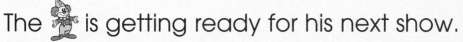 is getting ready for his next show.

Help him by drawing lines between the ⬤'s and the 👝's with matching numbers. Start with 1 and go in number order.

Good job! Place your star sticker here.
Now jump ahead to the next page.

Numerical Sequence (13)

This 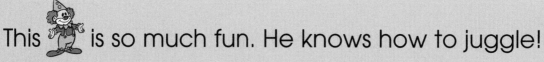 is so much fun. He knows how to juggle!

Draw lines between these numbers and their matching balls.

| 1 | 2 | 3 | 4 | 5 | 6 | 7 | 8 | 9 | 10 |

2   1   4   9   7

3   5   6   8   10

Can you count backwards? Look at the numbers along the top. Start with 10 and say each number counting back to 1.

Oh, no! This  is about to drop three bike ⊛'s.
Help him keep them in the air.

Write the missing numbers in order on the empty wheels.

Eleanor's Tips

Here's how to write the number **8**. Follow the arrows and trace along the lines.

We are bobbing for 🍎's!

Write the missing numbers so we can eat them all.

Up, up, and away! There goes Casey!

Write the missing numbers on the so he can get down.

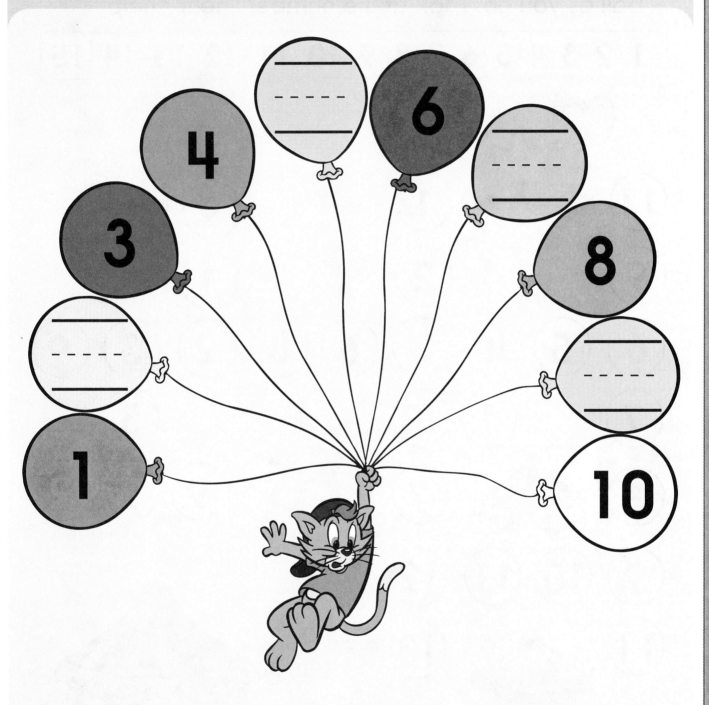

One of the tents has a . Pierre left us this path of balls to help us find our way to it.

Follow the path in order from 1 to 15 coloring each ball as you go. Look at the number line for help.

1 2 3 4 5 6 7 8 9 10 11 12 13 14 15

START

Eleanor's Tips

A good way to practice writing is with the eraser side of your pencil.

Whee! It's the number roller coaster.

Help me finish my ride by filling in the missing numbers. The numbers in the box will help you.

4	6	8	12	14	17	20

Let's ride horses and play this number game.

Say each number out loud. Then trace the number in each space until you reach the barn.

Circle the number that is your age.

Can you count backwards starting from 20? Say all the numbers on the path all the way back to 1.

5 6 7 8 9

18 19 20 Finish

Fantastic! Place a train sticker on your Certificate of Completion. Now jump ahead for more fun!

Review 21

Eleanor's Tips

It helps to count on your fingers. Then you can hold your hands up to show how many.

Lunchtime! How many 🍞's did we pack?

Count them by holding up one finger for each 🍞. Write the number on the line.

_____
- - - - -
_____

Shhhh! We're so tired!

How many of us are sleeping? Write the number on the line.

_____

Can you count how many sandwiches we have now? _____

Good job! Place your star sticker here. Now jump ahead to the next page.

Number Puzzles (23)

Kisha is trying to paint Casey's face like a clown!

Put an X on the picture with the same number of 's as the real Casey. Then color in the painting.

It's time for more fun on the 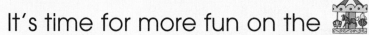.

In each row, circle the  with the number that matches the number of  we are holding.

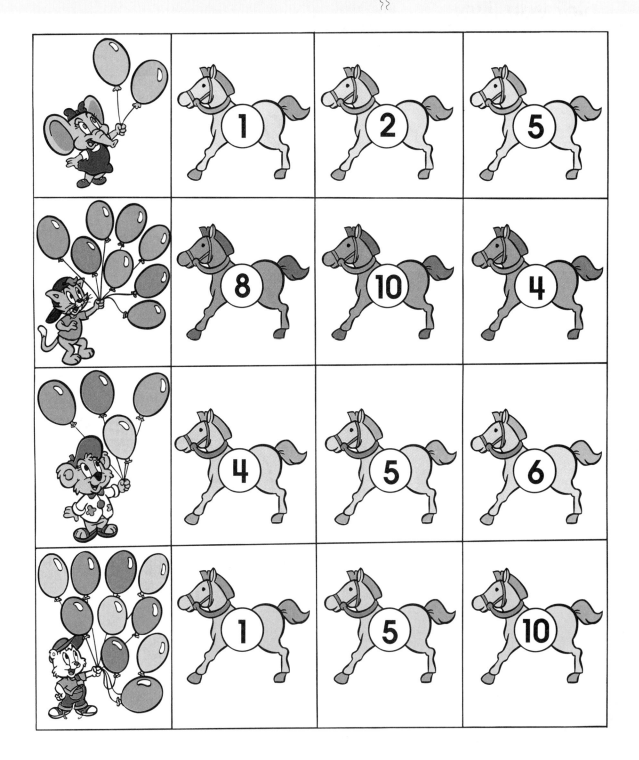

Level 2

Look at these tall 's!

Circle the tree with the same number of branches as the one on my map. Then color in the trees any color you like.

MAP

Casey's going to juggle everything in his backpack!

In each row, circle the number that tells how many of each thing he has.

How many flashlights? 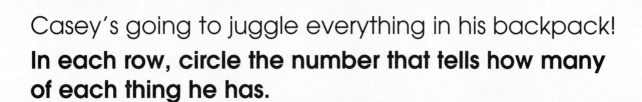	3	5	10
How many apples?	2	7	8
How many balls?	4	9	10
How many gloves?	1	3	7

Good job! Place your star sticker here.
Now jump ahead to the next page.

Number Puzzles **27**

Eleanor's Tips

Sometimes it's easier to count a lot of things when they are sorted into **groups**.

Look at that 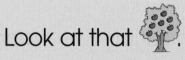.
Follow the directions below.

Color 5 🍎's red.
Color 5 🍎's green.
Color 5 🍎's blue.
Color 5 🍎's orange.

How many 🍎's in all?

_____

- - - - - - - - - -

_____

The 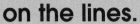 gave us these ▲'s to take home. Let's count them before we go.

Read the sentences below and write the answers on the lines.

 has _____ ▲'s.

 has _____ ▲'s.

How many 's in all? _____

Nice job! Place your star sticker here.
Now jump ahead to see what you've learned.

Number Puzzles **29**

It's almost time to go home, but first you can help Pierre win the -eating contest. Yummy!

How many 's? _____

How many 's? _____

How many have 's? _____

Write your answers to the questions below.

_____
- - - - - - - -
How many have 's? _____

_____
- - - - - - - -
How many have 🍒's? _____

On a separate piece of paper, draw your favorite ice cream treat!

Great work! Place a train sticker on your Certificate of Completion.

Review **31**

Answer Key

PAGE 2	draw line and color from 1 to 5	PAGE 15	write 3, 6, 9
PAGE 3	trace 3; circle third carousel	PAGE 16	write 1, 4, 8, 10
		PAGE 17	write 2, 5, 7, 9
PAGE 4	color the middle path	PAGE 18	color path circles in order from 1 to 15
PAGE 5	connect dots 1 to 10; color horse	PAGE 19	write 4, 6, 8, 12, 14, 17, 20
PAGE 6	connect 4/4, 2/2, 8/8, 10/10	PAGES 20-21	trace numbers 1 through 20; count backwards from 20
PAGE 7	draw line from 1 to 10		
PAGE 8	color horses 1, 2, 3 blue; 4, 5, 6 red; 7, 8, 9 green	PAGE 22	write 6
		PAGE 23	write 3; 2
		PAGE 24	X on third picture; color Casey
PAGE 9	connect dots 1 to 20; color clown	PAGE 25	circle 2, 8, 4, 10
PAGES 10-11	connect dots 1 to 20; 1 to 10; color pictures	PAGE 26	circle middle tree; color trees
PAGE 12	trace 2; say each number and color tickets	PAGE 27	circle 3, 7, 10, 1
		PAGE 28	color the apples; write 20
PAGE 13	connect 3/3, 1/1, 2/2, 5/5, 4/4	PAGE 29	write 5, 10, 15
PAGE 14	connect 1/1, 2/2, 3/3, 4/4, 5/5, 6/6, 7/7, 8/8, 9/9, 10/10; count backwards from 10	PAGES 30-31	write 6, 5, 1, 8, 15